This book is dedicated to my daughter, Rebekah.
I wanted to complete my doctorate before you were around,
and now I am glad that I did because I don't want to
miss a moment as you grow, explore, and learn.

Hopefully this guide will allow other parents pursuing degrees
to spend a little less time on the next paper
and a little more time with their children while pursuing their dreams.

In loving memory of Leroy H. Weiss, Jr.
1944-2015

Student Quick Reference Success Guide to Writing in the APA 6th Edition Style

Charles P. Kost II, Ed.D.

Important notice regarding book materials

ISBN: 978-1-329-13206-1

Charles P. Kost II, Ed.D.
Kost Services, LLC
PO Box 100
Presto, PA 15142

www.kostservices.com
chuck@kostservices.com

Ordering Information:

Quantity sales. Special discounts are available on quantity purchases by educators, associations, and others. For details, contact the publisher at: **http://www.lulu.com**.

Stock art was licensed through istockphoto.com, shutterstock.com and vectorstock.com.

Student Quick Reference Success Guide to Writing in the APA 6th Edition Style

Table of Contents

(Mechanics and Structure)

(Types of References)

Introduction

This book was developed to assist students in learning and implementing the basic components of writing in the APA style. The materials are designed to offer practical application of the basic rules as required by the American Psychological Association. This is not an exhaustive list of all of the rules, but a compilation of the most common mechanics that are required in the APA writing style.

Most topics in this booklet include the page number to reference a detailed description in the Publication Manual of the American Psychological Association, Sixth Edition (ISBN: 978-1-4338-0561-5), to allow the student to obtain further guidance, as needed. This booklet is not a replacement for the publication manual, but instead it is supplementary resource to save the student time and frustration.

General Paper Formatting

The purpose of standardized formatting is to ensure consistency and ease of reading for every document. Following the style guide allows others to instantly identify the authors that were referenced in the document and understand what is being conveyed in the document without having to decipher the mechanics of the writing. There are several standard components found on a typical page; most are addressed using a callout on the sample page below.

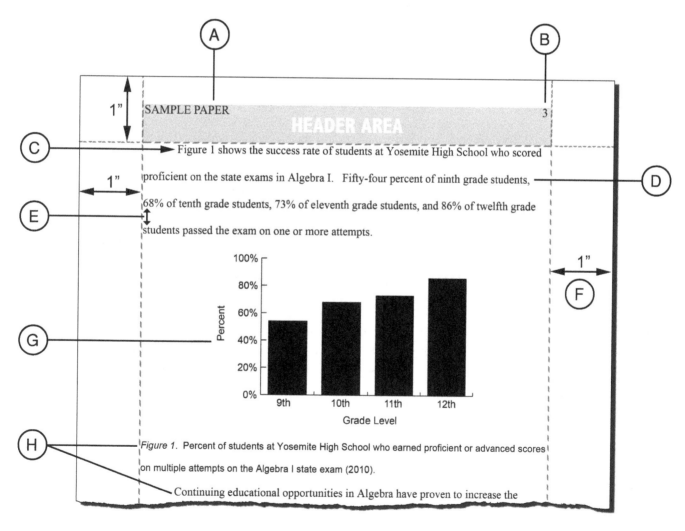

Margins Ⓕ: (p. 229) All pages should be 8.5 inches (wide) by 11 inches (tall) and margins on all pages should be one (1) inch. The use of a gutter (0.5 inches) for binding is permissible.

Font Ⓗ: (p. 228) Always use serif font (e.g., Time New Roman). The only exception to this is the use of a sans serif font (e.g., Arial or Helvetica) for all wording in figures. Regardless which font is required, the text size should always be 12-point.

Sentence Spacing Ⓔ: (p. 229) All parts of the paper should be double-spaced. This includes the titles, headings, figures, tables, abstract, appendices, and the reference list. Extra lines should not be added between paragraphs or new headings.

Text Alignment Ⓓ: (p. 229) All text should be left aligned except those specific headings that are centered. Right and full justification should not be used.

Indentation Ⓒ: (p. 229) The first line of every paragraph (except in the abstract or block quote) should be indented 5 spaces (equivalent to pressing the "tab" key once).

Punctuation Spacing: (p. 87) Place two spaces after each sentence in the text. One space should be placed after commas, semicolons, colons, and any period that is part of a citation or in the initials in a person's name. Spaces should not be used in abbreviations, for example: e.g., i.e., or p.m. When a colon is used to represent a ratio (e.g., 1:2), no space should antecede the colon.

Paragraph Length: Paragraphs should be at least three (3) sentences in length. As a general rule, paragraphs should never consist of only one sentence, but a paragraph should also not fill an entire page. Use sub-sections to divide long paragraphs. (See the section on headings.)

Page Numbers Ⓑ: (p. 230) Every page of the paper should have a page number. The title page serves as page one of your paper. Page numbers must appear in the upper right hand corner of the document. It should be located in the document header. **Exception**: The title page sometimes does not display a page number when a table of contents is included. In this case, the title page is numbered "i" (i.e., lowercase Roman numeral 1).

Header Ⓐ: (p. 230) On every page, except the first, the title is written in all capital letters. If the title is longer than fifty (50) characters (included spaces), then only the first fifty (50) characters are included. Additionally, subtitles (usually written after a colon) are not included. See the *Title Page* section to view how to setup the header.

Figures Ⓖ: (p. 150) Any figure (e.g., graph, picture, diagram, drawings, plot) in a paper must be sequentially numbered using Arabic numerals from first page to last. Before adding a figure to a paper, be sure that the figure is necessary to clearly articulate your point. Figures should use a sans serif font and all text should be clear and easy to read. Two-dimensional shapes are preferred to ensure readability. Introduce all figures in the text before they appear. Figures should be labeled, underneath the figure using the same font as the figure (typically a sans serif font: *Figure 1*: Descriptive Title.

Special Characters: (p. 229) Use the word processing special character selection for as many special characters as possible. Special characters include math symbols, Greek letters, and symbols.

Designed by Charles P. Kost II, Ed.D. Duplication Prohibited. © 2015 Kost Services, LLC

Tables

(p. 128) Any table that requires two or fewer columns or rows should be written as text. The following guidelines should be followed when creating a table. The table must be introduced in the text Ⓐ before it appears in the paper (p. 130). The table must fit within the margins of the paper Ⓕ; however, you will notice that the table lines extend past text margins; this is acceptable.

Organize the data in a meaningful way Ⓔ that allows the reader to compare the values for two or more groups next to each other, in either the columns or rows (p. 129). The entire table should be double-spaced. Format all compared numbers Ⓖ in the table the same way using the same number of digits (p. 137). Always use the same units of measure for values that are being compared.

Each table must have a title Ⓒ and headers Ⓓ for each column and/or row (p. 133). The traditional table only uses horizontal lines around the header and at the end of the table. Vertical lines are not used to separate columns. If the data in the table are from another source, include a citation for the original location of the data.

Tables are sequentially numbered Ⓑ using Arabic numerals from the first to last page (p. 127). Text in the table is formatted in the same font as the body of the text.

Ⓐ The dropout percentage of the first cohort that was calculated using the new formula was the graduating class of 2010; therefore, all prior data, listed in Table 3, uses the previously adopted formula.

Ⓑ Table 3

Ⓒ *Pennsylvania High School Dropout Rates*

School Year	Number of Dropouts	Secondary Enrollment	Dropout Rate
2001-02	18,584	849,994	2.2%
2002-03	18,560	863,771	2.1%
2003-04	16,986	877,021	1.9%
2004-05	17,178	882,908	1.9%
2005-06	16,829	889,226	1.9%

Ⓓ (points to header row) Ⓔ (points to data rows) Ⓕ 1" Ⓖ 1"

Statistical Tables: Most statistical tables have specific formatting requirements. Refer to the APA Manual for detailed information about statistical data.

The Title Page

The title page of any paper written in the APA style is the first page that readers will see. There are several components of the title page; each addressed using a callout on the sample page below. Title page formatting is more influenced by university requirements than the APA standards.

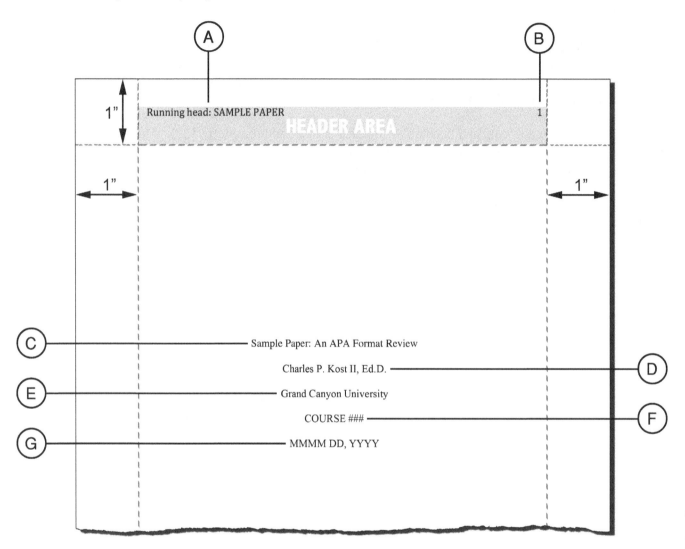

Running Head Ⓐ: (p. 230) A running head is located on the left in the header of the paper and includes the words "Running head:" on the title page. (On all additional pages, only the title after these words is included.) The running head is the basic title of the paper and it is written in all capital letters. If the title is longer than fifty (50) characters (included spaces), then only the first fifty (50) characters are included. Additionally, subtitles (usually written after a colon) are not included. In the sample page above, only the words *Sample Paper* are included in the running head. The subtitle *An APA Format Review* should be omitted.

Page Number Ⓑ: (p. 230) The first page of the paper is always the title page and should be labeled as page 1 on the right in the header.

Click <u>V</u>iew, and then <u>H</u>eader and Footer in Microsoft® Word® to enter the header and footer sections of the paper. To format the header, click on the Header and Footer ribbon that appears. Of particular note should be the "Different First Page" checkbox that allows the author to make the first page to look different from the remainder of the pages.

Title Block: (p. 23) The title block includes title of the paper Ⓒ on the first line, the author's name Ⓓ on the second line, the name of the university Ⓔ on the third line, the course number Ⓕ on the fourth line, and the date Ⓖ on the last line (e.g., Format: December 3, 2012). The title block should be double-spaced and vertically centered on the page. **Note**: Do not add earned degrees behind your name for papers that are written for a course. Formal papers may include degrees that were earned to show expertise. The title block may vary slightly from university to university.

Abstract

(p. 26 – 27) When an abstract is required, it is located on its own page, after the title page and before the first page of the paper (or a table of contents for longer papers). It contains the header Ⓐ and page number Ⓑ, which is usually page two. Centered at the top of the page Ⓒ is the word *Abstract* in standard text font (e.g., no italic or bold). The text of the abstract Ⓓ is a brief synopsis of the contents of the paper. Most universities and journals provide a limit for the length of the abstract, in the number of words. The abstract is the first page that most people read in order to decide if they should take the time to read the entire paper. References should be included sparingly on the Abstract page; it is a summary of the paper written, not others' works. For longer papers, a list of keywords Ⓔ is provided. The list starts after the abstract and is indented 0.5 inches with the word *Keywords* in italic followed by a colon and the keywords for the paper. These are the words that are identified for a search engine to find your paper if it is published.

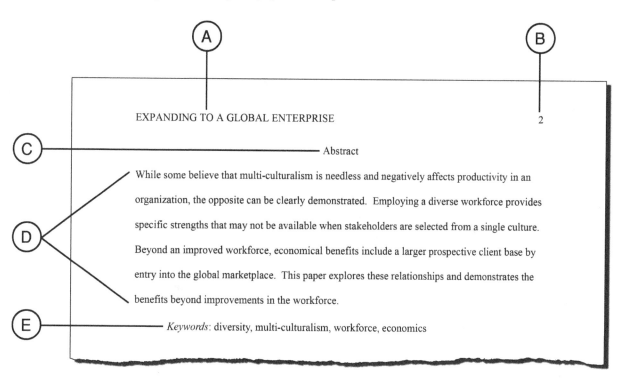

Headings

Headings (pp. 62 – 63) are used to organize the paper. There are a total of five headings categories; however, most papers do not require the use of all five heading levels. Longer papers tend to use more headings to properly organize the topics in the paper and shorter papers tend to require less heading levels. Think of headings as a basic outline of the paper. Topics that are similar or equally important should be included on the same level. More important topics are assigned Level I or Level II headings and topics that support these main ideas use Level III, IV, or V headings.

Each level has its own formatting requirements so the reader can distinguish between headings. Papers that are shorter in length typically utilize one or two heading levels. The figure below shows the hierarchy of the five levels as well as their formatting guidelines. The entire title appears as the first line of the paper (as it appears in the title block). The title is centered and does **not** count as a level one heading. The title is followed by an introduction to the paper. Since it is assumed that the first paragraph(s) of your paper are the introduction, the title *Introduction* is **never** used. The heading *Conclusion* should be last Level I heading and should include a summary of the findings in the paper.

When adding subheadings there must be at least two subheadings at the same level in the same part of the paper (e.g., two Level II sub-headings under the same Level I heading). Each heading must have at least a paragraph consisting of three (3) sentences. The last sentence of each section, regardless of level heading should transition the reader from the current section to the new section.

Paper Title	→ Centered, Upper and Lower Case
Centered, Bold, Upper and Lower Case Heading	← Level I
Left Justified, Bold, Upper and Lower Case Heading	← Level II
Indented, bold, lower case, paragraph heading ending with a period.	← Level III
Indented, bold, italics, lower case, paragraph heading ending with a period.	← Level IV
Indented, italics, lower case, paragraph heading ending with a period.	← Level V

The examples on the following pages illustrate the proper use of the heading levels in a paper context. Use these examples to clarify how your paper should look. Remember that you must use the heading levels in order. You cannot use a Level III heading unless it is inside a Level II heading section. For more complex papers, it may be beneficial to write the headings (in the proper format) for the entire paper and then write the body of the paper in the proper section. Add additional headings or delete headings that are not needed as you write.

Designed by Charles P. Kost II, Ed.D. Duplication Prohibited. © 2015 Kost Services, LLC

Sample Paper with One Level

Leadership Styles of School-Level Administrators ⟸ Paper Title

This paragraph is the introduction to the paper. This introduces the topic and briefly explains the intent and rationale of the paper. It includes a transition to the first Level I section.

Characteristics of Leadership Styles ⟸ Level I

This section includes information about the characteristics of each of the leadership styles (e.g., transformational, authoritarian, servant leadership) addressed in this paper. This includes a transition to the next Level I section.

Stakeholder Views of Administrator Leadership Styles ⟸ Level I

This section includes information about how each stakeholder (e.g., teachers, parents, students) respond to each leadership style. This includes a transition to the final Level I section.

Implications of Leadership Styles ⟸ Level I

This section includes the benefits and risks associated with using each leadership style. This includes a transition to the conclusion.

Conclusion ⟸ Level I

This section briefly summarizes the contents of the paper. The conclusion is considered a Level I heading.

Sample Paper with Two Levels

In the sample below, the same Level I headings were used as the previous example, but to clarify the leadership styles addressed in the paper (e.g., Transformational, Authoritarian, Servant Leadership) each was assigned a Level II heading under the *Characteristics of Leadership Styles*. A group of Level II headings under *Stakeholder Views of Administrator Leadership Styles* could also be added to organize that section of the paper as well. Then, a group of Level III headings could be placed under this Level II heading to address each leadership style if the paper was expanded.

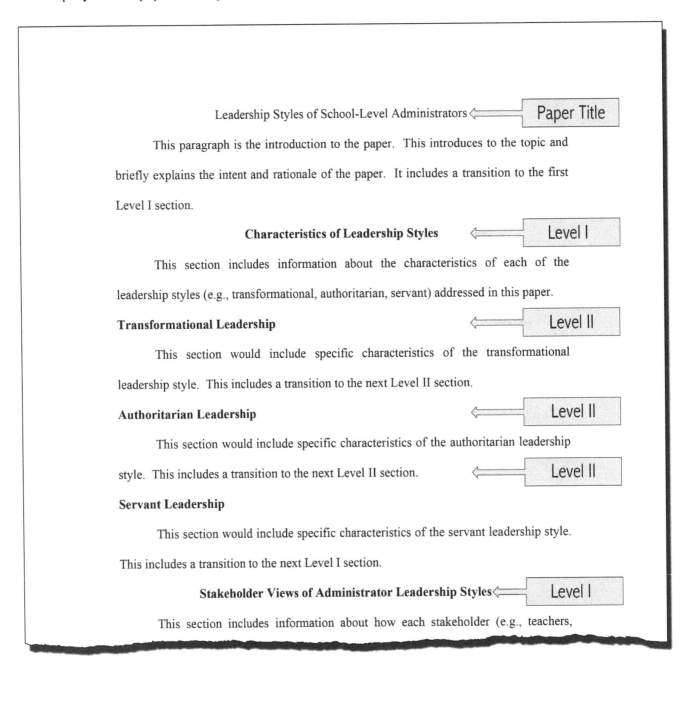

Mechanics and Structure

The section about General Paper Formatting beginning on page 1, provides information about setting up your paper. Common grammatical, mechanical, and structural issues that are addressed in the APA style guide are included in this section. These technical requirements assist writers in developing consistent works.

Commas in a Series: (p. 88) When using a series of three or more items, place a comma before the words *and/or* (e.g., …she had previously taken Algebra I, Geometry**,** and Algebra II).

Parentheses: (p. 94) Back to back parentheses are not permitted. Instead, include items in one set of parentheses separated by a semicolon. **For example**: …the junior high students (e.g., seventh and eighth grade; Smith, 2014). Parentheses for in-text citations should end inside the sentence terminator including explanation and question marks. **Example**: …grades (Smith, 2014).

Prepositions: A preposition typically indicates the location of a person or object. A sentence cannot end with a preposition (e.g., Incorrect: "Where are you from?" Correct: "Where do you reside?"). Rewrite sentences that end in a preposition.

Contractions: Contractions are typically used in informal conversation and writing. Avoid using contractions (e.g., don't, can't, doesn't) and instead write the words out (e.g., do not, cannot, does not).

Direct Quotes: (p. 170) Sometimes it is necessary to add direct quotes to a research paper. If the quote has less than 40 words, the quote can be added directly to your text. A citation and the page number where you found the reference is all that is needed Ⓑ. You can separate the author and date from the page number Ⓐ, to vary your writing.

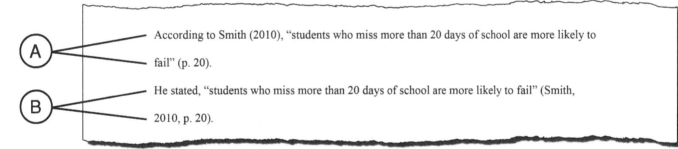

If a quote has more than 40 words, the quote must be formatted in its own freestanding block that is indented the standard one-half inch on all lines. The indentation indicates that the paragraph is a quote and therefore quotation marks are not used. Typically, some text will be required to introduce the quote. The sentence before the quote can end in a period or colon. The quote can be its own paragraph or it may be part of another. For example:

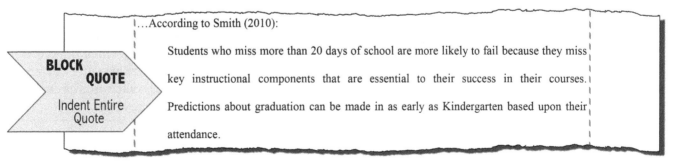

Use of Ampersands (&): (p. 175, 184) The word *and* should be used throughout the body of the paper except in in-text citations (in parentheses) and the reference section. Use the ampersand (&) instead of *and* in the citations (e.g., Smith & Ford, 2012). Use a semi-colon in a citation to separate two citations in the same set of parentheses. **For example**: (Greenleaf, 1977; Northouse, 2006) shows both references provided the same information.

Theories, Models, and Instruments: (p. 102) The names of theories (A) and models should not be capitalized. The names of instruments should be capitalized (B), but not the words *test* or *scale* for subscales of test of a larger instrument.

Anchors in Instruments: (p. 105) When describing the anchors used in scales (C) do not use quotation marks. The anchors should be written in italics.

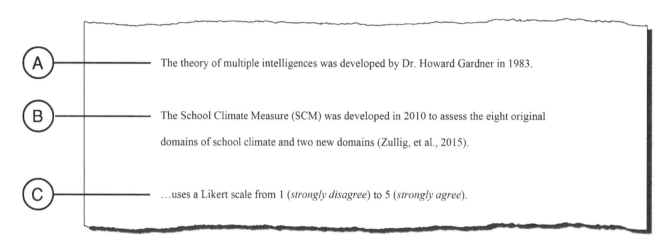

Acronyms: (p. 88) Acronyms should be spelled out completely in the initial appearance in the text. The abbreviation should appear in parentheses after that initial appearance. All subsequent appearances can then use the acronym in the parentheses.

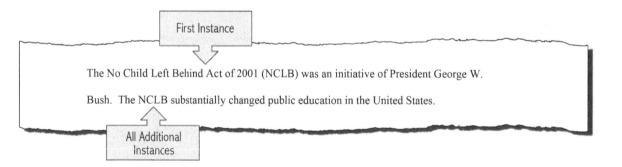

Abbreviations: (p. 108) Abbreviations should be used sparingly. While they can improve readability by keeping repetitive words to a minimum, too many abbreviations make reading the text more cumbersome. Like acronyms, abbreviations should include an explanation before their inclusion in the manuscript. Some common abbreviations are accepted as words (e.g., IQ, REM, ESP, AIDS, HIV, NADP, and ACTH) and do not need an explanation.

Footnotes and Endnotes: (p. 37) APA does not recommend the use of footnotes or endnotes. However, if footnotes are necessary to illustrate your point, a superscript numeral should follow any punctuation mark. The footnote should use the same superscript font and appear at the bottom of the same page. If you use endnotes, a separate page should appear after your reference page with the title *Footnotes* centered at the top of the page. Type each footnote in standard text form, indenting the first line.

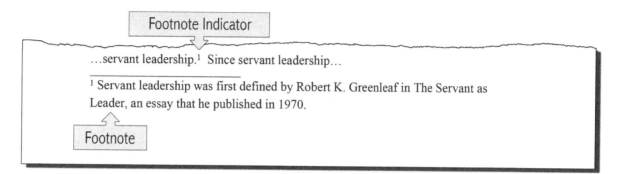

Latin Abbreviations: (p. 108) Latin abbreviations are permitted when writing in the APA style. The four common allowable and one forbidden abbreviation are outlined below.

e.g., - this means "for example" and is always written inside parentheses and in lower case. Each letter is followed by a period and the last period is followed by a comma. **Example**: The stakeholders (e.g., parents, teachers, students) are...

i.e., - this means "that is" and is always written inside parentheses and in lower case. Each letter is followed by a period and the last period is followed by a comma. **Example**: The person in charge (i.e., the principal or other designee by the superintendent...)

et al., - this means "and others" and is always written in lower case. Notice there is no period after "et". This can be used in the body of the paper and is common in any citation with more than two authors **after** the first time it appears in the paper. **Example**: ...students made academic improvements (Smith, James, Johnson, & Cohen, 2012)...According to Smith et al., (2012) the students...

etc... - this is the abbreviation for etcetera, meaning "a list that is too tedious to give in full." Avoid using this in formal writing. Research papers are one place that all items should be listed.

vs. – this abbreviation means "versus" or "against" and is written in the text in lower case. **Example**: Wyoming vs. Montana describes the differences between the states. **Exception**: Court cases use v. to represent the word versus. **Example**: In Brown v. Board of Education...

Lists: (p. 63) Lists can be included in manuscripts. Lists within a sentence can be listed using letters or numbers Ⓐ. Bulleted or numbered lists can be used and each item must be followed by a comma, semicolon, or period depending on grammatical structure Ⓑ.

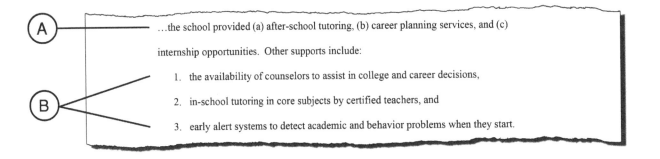

Ⓐ …the school provided (a) after-school tutoring, (b) career planning services, and (c) internship opportunities. Other supports include:

Ⓑ
1. the availability of counselors to assist in college and career decisions,
2. in-school tutoring in core subjects by certified teachers, and
3. early alert systems to detect academic and behavior problems when they start.

Writing Style

The style of your writing is as important as the mechanics used to format your work. Consistency in writing style improves readability of your work. Your writing should be as precise and succinct as possible, even when a specific word count is required.

Paraphrasing: (pp. 15 – 16 & 170 – 174) It is necessary to paraphrase, or rewrite someone else's ideas in your own words. Anytime another work is referenced, it is necessary to properly cite the work so others know which ideas are yours and which came from other sources. Failure to do so is a form of plagiarism and disciplinary action can be taken when it is found, even after graduation.

Passive Voice: (p. 26 & 77) Verbs are classified as either passive or active voice. Since passive voice tends to avoid responsibility by making it sound as if the subject (noun) of the sentence is not completing the action (verb), it should not be used in research.

> **Active Voice**: The school board approved the new rule.
> **Passive Voice**: The new rule was approved by the school board.

It is preferred that passive voice is not used in APA style writing. Microsoft® Word® has a feature that will underline passive voice phrases to assist you as you write.

Redundancy: Repeated use, or overuse, of the same word or words takes away from the quality of the writing. Change overused words to different words with the same meanings (e.g. synonyms), but use care to ensure that the new words have the same meaning. Redundant language states the same thing twice in the same sentence. Below are examples common phrases that are redundant. You can read each statement with and without the word in bold and arrive at the same conclusion.

- There were **a total of** 24 participants in the study.
- It has been **previously** discovered by Smith (2012) that…
- It was **absolutely** essential to the success of the study.

Anthropomorphism: (p. 68) Anthropomorphism is giving a human characteristic (e.g., qualities, attributes, or actions) to a non-human item (e.g., animal, object, research paper). The most common anthropomorphism in research are: "The research shows" or "The data suggest."

Formatting Numbers

(p. 111) Numbers between one (1) and nine (9) should be written out in words (e.g., there were five items on the survey) unless followed by unit of measurement (e.g., 12 inches). Numbers greater than or equal to 10 should be typed in numerical form (e.g., 10, 199, 2,567). Numbers, not words, should always be used to represent dates, decimals (e.g., 4.25), percentages (e.g., 49%), ratios (e.g., 4 of 6 students), statistical functions, and reference to a specific location in the paper (e.g., chapter 3, section 12, page 94). Common expressions including twenty-first century and the Fourth of July should be written as words. All numbers in the abstract of a paper should be written numerically. Anytime two values are written next to each other (e.g., the survey consisted of five 10-point Likert scale questions), use a combination of words and numerals. When writing the plural of numbers (e.g., 1960s or nines) do not use apostrophes before the "s."

Decimal Values: (p. 113) All decimal values (e.g., values $0 < x < 1$) should be written with a zero preceding the value (e.g., 0.5) and all trailing zeroes should be removed – unless written in a table, then the same number of decimal places should be written for all compared values. Omit the preceding 0 for statistical values (e.g., $p < .05$).

Fractions: (p. 123) Fractions should be written in text form (e.g., instead of ½ write *one half*). Do not use a hyphen unless the fraction is being used as a compound adjective (e.g., the senate needs a two-thirds majority to advance the bill).

Percentages: (p. 118) Percentages should be written as a numerical value with a percent sign (%). **For example**: 4% not 4 percent. However, if you start a sentence with a percentage, then the words should be spelled out (e.g., Sixty-five percent of the students…).

Roman Numerals: (p. 118) Roman numerals are only used for established terminology (e.g., Type II Error).

Large Values: (p. 114) When possible, use a combination of words and numerals to express the values (e.g., 15.2 trillion dollars) or if exact values are required, use commas every three (3) places starting from the decimal point location (e.g., $15,245,432,193). Page numbers, binary numbers, serial numbers, temperatures, audio frequencies, and degrees of freedom are not grouped using commas.

Measures of Time: (p. 108) All measures of time should be written in numeric form (e.g., 1:30 P.M.; 4 hours and 32 minutes; between the 5th and 20th of May; May 15, 2013).

Common Measurement Abbreviations: (p. 108 & 115) It is permissible to use abbreviations for units of measure. Common abbreviations are provided below.

Measure	Abbreviation
Degrees Centigrade	°C
Degrees Fahrenheit	°F
Hour(s)	h
Minute(s)	min
Second(s)	s
Millisecond(s)	ms
Reaction Time	RT
Kilometers per Hour	kph
Intelligence Quotient	IQ

Measure	Unit (Abbreviation)
Weight	Grams (g)
Distance/Length	Meters (m)
Volume	Liters (l)

Metric Units*	Abbreviation
milli	m
centi	c
hecto	h
kilo	k

* must be used with one of the measure abbreviations. For example: mm for millimeter.

Reporting Statistics

There are specific formatting requirements for reporting statistics in the APA style. Specifically, spacing and the use of italics should be strictly followed. For more information about adding statistics to your paper, review pages 116 to 124 in the APA manual. Some basic formatting is provided below.

Statistical Values: (p. 116) All statistical values should be written in numerical form (e.g., 12 out of 15 participants; the sample size was 24). Except for p values, values should be rounded to two (2) decimal places (e.g., $p < .24$).

Statistical Variables: (p. 119) Most statistical symbols and abbreviations are written in italics. The most common are included below.

Symbol	Name/Description
ANCOVA	Analysis of Covariance
ANOVA	Analysis of Variance
α	Alpha
β	Beta
CI	Confidence Interval
d	Cohen's Measure
df	Degrees of Freedom
F	F-Ratio
F_{max}	Hartley's Fmax Test
H_a	Alternative Hypothesis
H_o	Null Hypothesis
MANOVA	Multivariate Analysis of Variance
$\bar{X}$ (or M)	Mean
Mdn	Median
MS	Mean Square
MSE	Mean Square Error
μ	Population Mean
n	Population of a Subgroup of a Sample
N	Total Number (Population) of the Sample
ns	Not Significant
p	Probability
σ	Sigma (Standard Deviation of the Population)
r	Pearson's Correlation
r^2	Coefficient of Determination
R	Multiple Correlation
s	Standard Deviation of the Sample
s^2	Sample Variance
SD	Standard Deviation
SE	Standard Error
SS	Sum of Squares
Σ	(Sigma) Sum
t	T-Test Value
χ^2	Chi Square Test Value
z	Z-Score

Significance Levels: Significance levels are reported using an italic *p* followed by a space and then the inequality sign followed by the value (e.g., $p > .05$). APA style requires reporting the exact *p* value in the text of the manuscript unless the *p* value is less than .001.

Mean and Standard Deviation: These calculations usually appear together Ⓐ in the same set of parentheses but can be separated if only one of the measurements are needed Ⓑ.

***t*-Tests**: For a *t*-test the degrees of freedom are in parentheses. This precedes the *t* statistic and the significance level Ⓒ.

ANOVA: Both one-way and two-way ANOVAs Ⓓ are reported like *t*-tests; however, there are two degrees of freedom. The degrees of freedom between groups is listed first, then a comma is inserted, and then the degrees of freedom within the groups is listed. This precedes the *F* statistics and the significance level.

Correlations: Report correlations Ⓔ with the degrees of freedom in parentheses and the significance level.

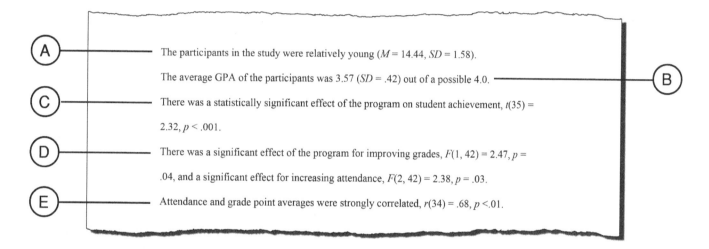

The participants in the study were relatively young ($M = 14.44$, $SD = 1.58$).

The average GPA of the participants was 3.57 ($SD = .42$) out of a possible 4.0.

There was a statistically significant effect of the program on student achievement, $t(35) = 2.32$, $p < .001$.

There was a significant effect of the program for improving grades, $F(1, 42) = 2.47$, $p = .04$, and a significant effect for increasing attendance, $F(2, 42) = 2.38$, $p = .03$.

Attendance and grade point averages were strongly correlated, $r(34) = .68$, $p < .01$.

Regression: Regression results are usually presented in a table; however, it is possible to include the results in your manuscript text. At a minimum, the slope, t-test value, corresponding significance level, degrees of freedom, and percentage of variable should be included. The number of required items is the reason that the results are usually in a table.

Graphs and Plots: Statistical graphs and plots are displayed in the same manner as any other figure and must be labeled as a figure.

Statistical Tables: (p. 133) Most statistical tables have specific formatting requirements. Refer to the APA Manual for detailed information about statistical data.

Biased Language

(p. 71) In academic writing, minimizing the use of biased language is important. Eliminating biased language in writing reduces misinterpretation and increases the author's credibility. There are several guidelines provided in the APA style guide to reduce the use of biased language.

Gender: (p. 73) Gender specific pronouns should be avoided. "He" should never be used as a generic pronoun. Writing should be completed in a way that gender-specific pronouns are not required. Avoid using *he/she* or *he or she* as these make the paper more difficult to read.

Ethnic and Racial Groups: (p. 75) All names of ethnic and racial groups (e.g., *Black, White, American Indian*) should be capitalized. Hyphens should not be used in group names (e.g., *African American* not *African-American*). As a general rule, racial groups classify people by similar physical characteristics and ethnic groups share a common genealogy. Avoid biased language about ethnic and racial groups (e.g., do not refer to *non-whites* as a *minority*).

Age: (p. 76) The terms boy and girl are reserved for people who are under 18 years of age. The term man and woman are used for people 18 and older. The term *older person* should be used instead of the word *elderly*.

Disabilities: (p. 76) The use of the term handicap should be used only to describe the source of the disability. To describe a person with a disability, use the terms: *person with Alzheimer's disease* or *person living with dementia*.

Common Word Errors

Affect vs. Effect: *Affect* is a noun that means *feeling or emotion*. As a verb, affect means *to act on* or *influence*. **For example**: Student attendance affects student grades. *Effect* is a noun that means the *outcome* or *consequence*. When used as a verb, it means to *cause to happen*. **For example**: An effect of not attending school is lower grades.

Data: (p. 96) While the word *data* appears to be singular; it is a plural word meaning a *body of facts* or *more than one datum*. As such, the proper usage in a sentence requires the use of plural verbs and descriptors. **For example**: "The data are…" and not "The data is…"

Impacted: The noun *impact* is appropriate to use (e.g., The impact of the study is…). However, the verb *impacted* is often misused. Unless you are writing about dental work (e.g., His tooth was impacted.), the word *impacted* should be replaced with *influenced* or *caused*.

That, Which, vs. Who: (p. 83) *Who* is used to refer to a person; never use *that* to refer to a person. *That* can be used to refer to an item. *Which* can be used to introduce a new clause (e.g., He improved his attendance, which in turn improved his grades.).

While vs. Although: (p. 84) *While* infers that events are occurring at the same time (e.g., the baby was born *while* the father was out of town). *Although* means "even though" and should appear in your paper more than the word *while* (e.g., although attendance usually predicts whether a student will graduate, that is not always the case).

Introduction to Citations and References

Citing work that is not your own in your paper is a vital aspect of using the APA Style for writing research papers. It serves two purposes. First, including citations shows the reading where the ideas in your paper were found. In turn, this allows research to build upon previously published works to continually improve and grow knowledge. If people did not share their research, many people would unknowingly produce the same research instead of building upon the work of others. Secondly, citing your works give proper credit for ideas that are not yours. This allows readers of your paper to go back to the works that you referenced to read other works about the same topic. In general, the in-text citation tells the reader whose work is represented by the preceding text and which reference in the reference list at the end of your paper can be used to find the source. The reader can use the reference list to find the same reference and view that document. Not properly citing where ideas in your research are from is considered plagiarism.

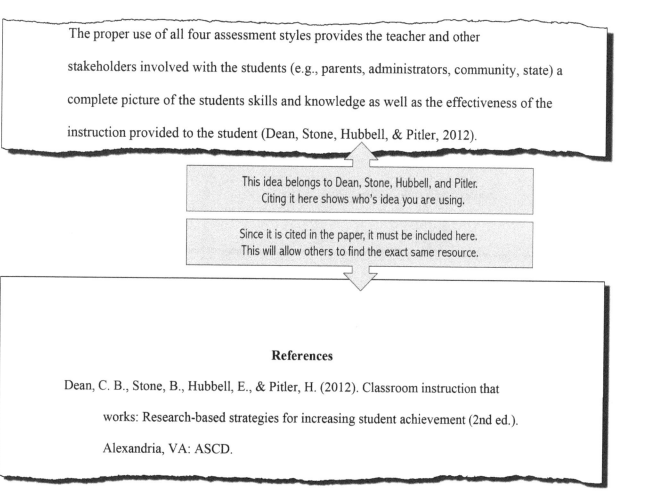

The proper use of all four assessment styles provides the teacher and other stakeholders involved with the students (e.g., parents, administrators, community, state) a complete picture of the students skills and knowledge as well as the effectiveness of the instruction provided to the student (Dean, Stone, Hubbell, & Pitler, 2012).

This idea belongs to Dean, Stone, Hubbell, and Pitler.
Citing it here shows who's idea you are using.

Since it is cited in the paper, it must be included here.
This will allow others to find the exact same resource.

References

Dean, C. B., Stone, B., Hubbell, E., & Pitler, H. (2012). Classroom instruction that works: Research-based strategies for increasing student achievement (2nd ed.). Alexandria, VA: ASCD.

For papers of longer length, the use of notation software, like Endnote®, can organize your references, include the proper citations in the body of the paper and format the references automatically. Additionally, websites like Citation Machine (www.citationmachine.net) can format your references and citations for you after you enter all required information. Finally, many online libraries, like the school's library, offer properly formatted references and a small download that imports your references into notation software. Caution should be used when using a preformatted reference as some libraries do not properly format the reference.

Citations

Citations (pp. 174 – 179) are fairly straightforward to include in your paper. Whenever you refer to another work, including but not limited to journal articles, books, websites, publications, or even your own previously published works, a citation must be included after that information is presented. This includes tables, diagrams, and figures, also. A basic citation includes the authors' name and the year of publication.

Single Author

(p. 174) As shown below, there are two ways to cite as your write. The first method Ⓐ is to place the author's last name or the organization's name in parentheses, followed by a comma and the date of publication. The second method Ⓑ includes the author's name (full or last only) or the organization's name in the sentence and then includes the date in parentheses with the name or at the end of the sentence. When the parentheses are at the end of the sentence, the parentheses with the citation are placed inside the punctuation mark at the end of the sentence. In the example below, The Center on Poverty, Employment, and Economics could be written out each time it appears or in the first instance of the citation, it could include its abbreviation in square brackets (e.g., The Center on Poverty, Employment, and Economics [CPEE]) and then the abbreviation CPEE can be used in all subsequent instances.

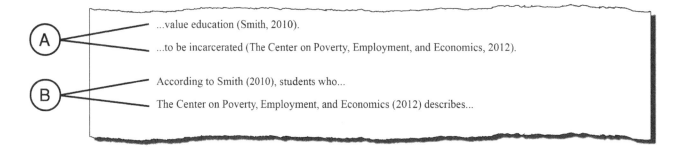

Multiple Authors

(p. 175) Citations that involve two or more authors are formatted slightly differently. For two (2) authors Ⓒ, list the last names of both authors with an ampersand (&) between the names. Follow this by a comma and the year of publication. This is repeated throughout the document whenever the citation is required. For three (3) or more authors Ⓓ, the first time the citation appears, list all of the authors followed by a comma and the year of publication. Each additional instance of the same reference is abbreviated (second line of Ⓓ) using only the first author's last name followed by a comma, then *et al*. Either format, as shown for one author can be used for multiple authors.

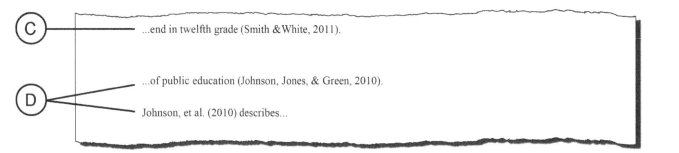

Works without Authors

(p. 176) If a citation is required for a source that does not have an author, use the first three (3) words of the title, as shown below Ⓔ in place of the author's name. Works listed as anonymous Ⓕ should be listed with the word *Anonymous*, followed by a comma and the publication year.

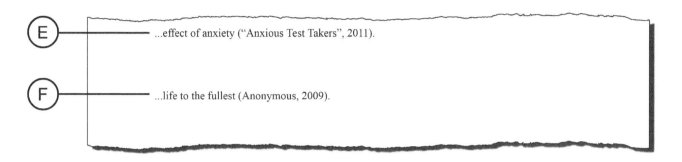

Ⓔ ...effect of anxiety ("Anxious Test Takers", 2011).

Ⓕ ...life to the fullest (Anonymous, 2009).

Specific Parts of a Source

(p. 179) When direct quotes are included in your work, the page number of the location of the quote in the source should be included so the reader can find the direct quote quickly in the original reference. You can also include page numbers in your citations for important information that is not written in your paper as a quote. When a page number is required Ⓖ, it is included after the date inside the in-text citation. Place a comma, then *p.* if the information is found on one page or *pp.* if it is found on multiple pages. The page number(s) are then included. You can reference the author in your paper and include the page number and date in one of two ways Ⓗ. Notice that when quotation marks are used, they are around the quote but not the citation. Place one space after the ending quotation mark, followed by the citation and then a period to end the sentence.

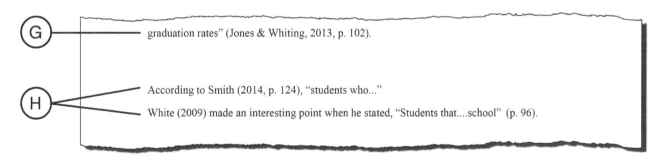

Ⓖ graduation rates" (Jones & Whiting, 2013, p. 102).

Ⓗ According to Smith (2014, p. 124), "students who..."

White (2009) made an interesting point when he stated, "Students that....school" (p. 96).

Secondary Sources

(p. 178) While primary sources are preferred, it is permissible to use a secondary source in your manuscript. Include the name of the original work, but credit the secondary source using a standard citation and corresponding reference.

Smith's study (as cited in Jones & Beaker, 2010) determined...

Reference List

The reference list (pp. 180 – 192) is a one-location list of all of sources that you referred to in your paper. There are several basic guidelines that should be followed when creating your reference list. These general requirements are outlined through the example below, regardless of the type of references used in your paper.

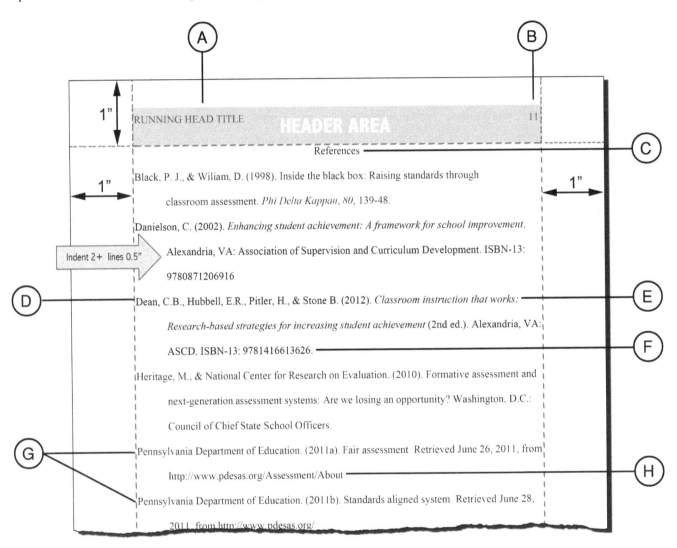

Header: Like all other pages in your document, this page has the running head title Ⓐ and page number Ⓑ in the header.

Margins: Page margins should be one (1) inch on all sides.

Title: The word *References* (no bold or italic) should appear center at the top of the page Ⓒ. The word *References* is considered a Level I heading when a table of contents is included.

Text Format: All text should be doubled spaced in Times New Roman font with 12-point size. The exception is that titles of journals (not journal articles) and books should be in italics Ⓔ. The list is left justified and to aid in reading, **all** lines after the first are indented 0.5 inches.

Location: The reference page is the last page of the document, unless appendices or endnotes are included.

Designed by Charles P. Kost II, Ed.D. Duplication Prohibited. © 2015 Kost Services, LLC

Page Organization: (p. 181) All references are listed in alphabetical order by the author's last name or the organization's name. If the author's name is not provided, the title of the source is then used to determine its place in the list, alphabetically. If multiple references are from the same author, use the date, and then title if the dates are the same to order the works.

Author: (p. 184) Authors names are formatted last name Ⓓ, followed by first and middle initials (e.g., Smith, J. T. for John Tony Smith or Jones, G. for Gregory Jones). List authors in the same order as they appear on the title page (i.e., authors are listed in order of contributions to the paper). If an editor's name is included as an author, the abbreviation (Eds.) is included after the name of the editor (e.g., White, N. T. (Eds.)).

Title: (p. 185) Only the first word Ⓔ of a title or subtitle should be capitalized (e.g., Living in poverty: An exploration of conditions). The exception to this is the use of formal names in a title (e.g., *Merriam-Webster's collegiate dictionary*). Titles of journal names (e.g., *New England Journal of Medicine*) or books (e.g., *An Elementary Approach to Statistics*) should be in italic. All other titles including the article or journal article titles should be non-italic.

Reference Page Numbers: (p. 179) When page numbers are required, single page numbers are preceded by a single *p* and a period (e.g., p. 123) and multiple pages are preceded by two *p*'s and a period (e.g., pp. 342-389).

Editions: If a reference has different editions, note the edition in parentheses (e.g., *Merriam-Webster's collegiate dictionary* (12th ed.)).

Volume and Issue Numbers: (p. 180) Volume numbers should appear in italics. Issue numbers follow the volume numbers in parentheses (e.g., *4*(3) represents Volume 4, Issue 3). Always use Arabic numerals even if Roman numerals are provided.

Dates: (p. 185) Most references are identified by the year of publication (e.g., 2013). Only certain citations use a full date in the format (YEAR, Month #) or (2010, July 4). If two or more sources are from the same author in the same year Ⓖ use small letters (e.g., a, b, c,...) with the date in both the reference and in-text citation (e.g., (Pennsylvania Department of Education, 2011a)) to distinguish between sources.

Web Addresses: (p. 188) All websites should have the "hyperlink" removed. This means it should not be colored differently than the rest of the text or underlined Ⓗ. To remove a hyperlink, place your cursor at the end of the web address and press backspace once. If this does not work, you can always remove the underline and change the font color to black.

ISBN and DOI Numbers: (p. 188) Printed publications are identified by a unique 10-digit (for older books) or 13-digit ISBN (International Standard Book Number). Electronic publications also have a unique identification number called a DOI (Digital Object Identifier). Whenever these numbers are available, they should be included in the reference citation to assist readers in finding the same sources Ⓕ.

Abbreviations: (p. 180) The common acceptable abbreviations in the reference list include:

Abbreviation	Description	Abbreviation	Description
ed.	Edition	Vol. (Vols.)	Volume(s)
Rev. ed.	Revised Edition	No.	Number
Ed. (Eds.)	Editor(s)	Pt.	Part
n.d.	No Date	Tech. Rep.	Technical Report

Types of References

There are many types of references (p. 173) that can be included in research papers. Only the most common are included in this guide. The general format is provided for each type. The letters correspond to an example located on the diagram below. For additional types of resources, refer to the APA manual.

Books (pp. 202 – 205)

One Author Ⓐ

Author, A. (Year). *Title*. City, State: Publisher. ISBN-13: #############

Two or More Authors Ⓑ

Author, A. & Author, B. (Year). *Title*. City, State: Publisher. ISBN-13: #############

Author, A., Author, B., & Author, C. (Year). *Title*. City, State: Publisher. ISBN-13: #############

No Author Ⓒ

Title (Edition Number). (Year). City, State: Publisher. ISBN-13: #############

Corporate Author Ⓓ

Organization Name. (Year). *Title*. City, State: Publisher. ISBN-13: #############

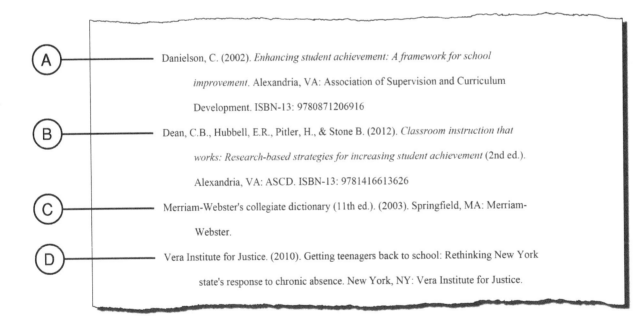

Ⓐ Danielson, C. (2002). *Enhancing student achievement: A framework for school improvement*. Alexandria, VA: Association of Supervision and Curriculum Development. ISBN-13: 9780871206916

Ⓑ Dean, C.B., Hubbell, E.R., Pitler, H., & Stone B. (2012). *Classroom instruction that works: Research-based strategies for increasing student achievement* (2nd ed.). Alexandria, VA: ASCD. ISBN-13: 9781416613626

Ⓒ Merriam-Webster's collegiate dictionary (11th ed.). (2003). Springfield, MA: Merriam-Webster.

Ⓓ Vera Institute for Justice. (2010). Getting teenagers back to school: Rethinking New York state's response to chronic absence. New York, NY: Vera Institute for Justice.

Journal Articles (pp. 198 – 199)

Journal articles are typically peer-reviewed research papers that are submitted to a journal for publication. These references must include the journal title, volume number (represented by "V" in the general form below), issue number (represented by "I" and if applicable), and page numbers of the article.

One Author, Accessed Online ⒠

Author, A. (Year). Article Title: Subtitle. Journal, *V*(I), page-page. DOI: ########

Two or More Authors, Accessed Online ⒡

Author, A. & Author, B. (Year). Article Title: Subtitle. Journal, *V*(I), start page – end page. DOI: ########

Author A., Author, B., & Author, C. (Year). Article Title: Subtitle. *Journal*, *V*(I), page-page. DOI: ########

Journal from Subscription Database – No DOI ⒢

Author, A. (Year, Month or Date). Article Title: Subtitle. *Journal*, V(I), start page – end page. Retrieved from

 Database Name. Retrieved from http://webaddress.com

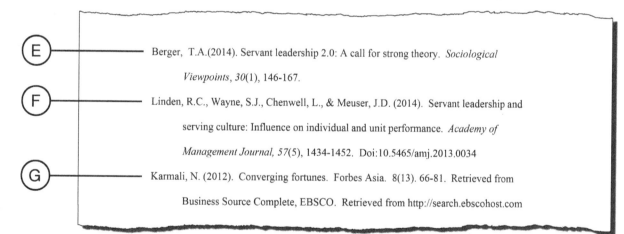

Ⓔ Berger, T.A.(2014). Servant leadership 2.0: A call for strong theory. *Sociological*

 Viewpoints, 30(1), 146-167.

Ⓕ Linden, R.C., Wayne, S.J., Chenwell, L., & Meuser, J.D. (2014). Servant leadership and

 serving culture: Influence on individual and unit performance. *Academy of*

 Management Journal, 57(5), 1434-1452. Doi:10.5465/amj.2013.0034

Ⓖ Karmali, N. (2012). Converging fortunes. Forbes Asia. 8(13). 66-81. Retrieved from

 Business Source Complete, EBSCO. Retrieved from http://search.ebscohost.com

Periodicals (pp. 200 – 202)

Newspaper Article, One Author – In Print Ⓗ

Author, A. (Year, Month, Day). Title: Subtitle. *Newspaper Name*, p. page.

Newspaper Article, Two or More Authors – In Print Ⓘ

Author, A. & Author, B. (Year, Month, Day). Title: Subtitle. *Newspaper Name*, p. page.

Author A., Author, B., & Author, C. (Year, Month, Day). Title: Subtitle. *Newspaper Name*, p. page.

NOTE: For all newspaper articles, if the article is continued on a second page, use the pp. designation with the page numbers separated by a comma (e.g., pp. A1, A10).

Magazine Article – In Print Ⓙ

Author, A. (Year, Moth, Day). Title. *Magazine Name*, *V*(I), start-page, end-page.

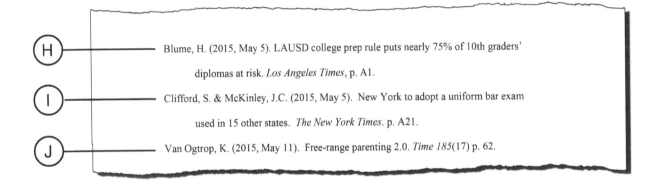

Ⓗ   Blume, H. (2015, May 5). LAUSD college prep rule puts nearly 75% of 10th graders'

        diplomas at risk. *Los Angeles Times*, p. A1.

Ⓘ   Clifford, S. & McKinley, J.C. (2015, May 5). New York to adopt a uniform bar exam

        used in 15 other states. *The New York Times*. p. A21.

Ⓙ   Van Ogtrop, K. (2015, May 11). Free-range parenting 2.0. *Time 185*(17) p. 62.

Research Reports and Dissertations (pp. 205 – 207)

Dissertations – Accessed Online Ⓚ

Author, A. (Year). Title (Doctoral dissertation). Available from ProQuest Dissertations and Theses database.

    (UMI No. ########)

NOTE: ProQuest is the publisher of **most** dissertations. If the dissertation or thesis is published through another publisher, replace the name of the publisher and UMI No. with the information provided for the DOI.

Government Report – Accessed Online Ⓛ

Government Department or Agency. (Year). *Title: Subtitle* (publication No. #########). City, State: Author.

    Retrieved from http://www.webaddress.com

Technical or Research Reports – Accessed Online Ⓜ

Author, A. (Year). *Title* (Number If Provided). City, State: Organization. Retrieved Month Day, Year, from

    http://www.webaddress.com

NOTE: Due to the variety of types of reports, these citations may vary. In the example below, the words "Research Brief" follow the title.

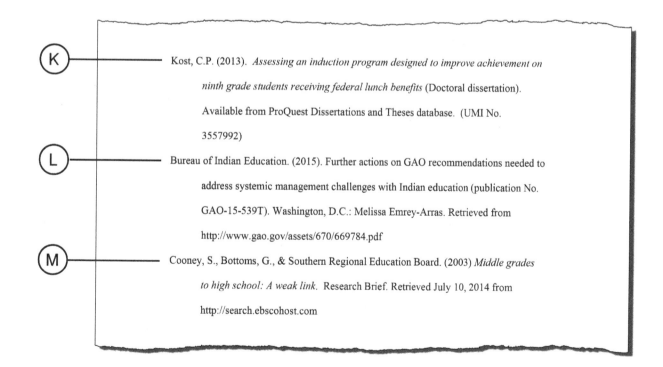

Ⓚ   Kost, C.P. (2013). *Assessing an induction program designed to improve achievement on ninth grade students receiving federal lunch benefits* (Doctoral dissertation). Available from ProQuest Dissertations and Theses database. (UMI No. 3557992)

Ⓛ   Bureau of Indian Education. (2015). Further actions on GAO recommendations needed to address systemic management challenges with Indian education (publication No. GAO-15-539T). Washington, D.C.: Melissa Emrey-Arras. Retrieved from http://www.gao.gov/assets/670/669784.pdf

Ⓜ   Cooney, S., Bottoms, G., & Southern Regional Education Board. (2003) *Middle grades to high school: A weak link.* Research Brief. Retrieved July 10, 2014 from http://search.ebscohost.com

Websites (pp. 214 – 215)

Care must be used when referencing websites and materials found online. Although many people believe that Wikipedia is a good place to get an idea about a particular topic, it should never be cited as a source in academic writing. Just like Wikipedia pages, websites can be written by anyone, including people who are not authorities on the subject being addressed.

Professional Website Ⓝ

Organization. (Year). *Title*. Retrieved Month Day, Year, from http://www.webaddress.com

Data Set from a Website Ⓞ

Author, A. (Year). *Title*. Retrieved Month Day, Year from Database Name database.

Organization. (Year). *Title* [statistics]. Available from Database Name database.

Blog Entry Ⓟ

Author, A. (Year, Month Day). Title. Message posted to http://www.webaddress.com

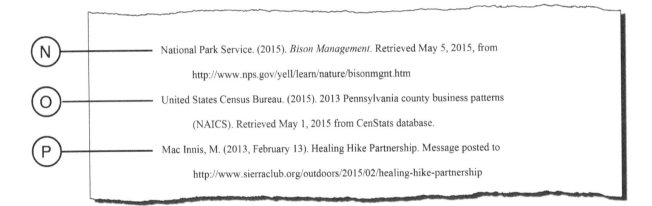

Ⓝ National Park Service. (2015). *Bison Management*. Retrieved May 5, 2015, from

http://www.nps.gov/yell/learn/nature/bisonmgnt.htm

Ⓞ United States Census Bureau. (2015). 2013 Pennsylvania county business patterns

(NAICS). Retrieved May 1, 2015 from CenStats database.

Ⓟ Mac Innis, M. (2013, February 13). Healing Hike Partnership. Message posted to

http://www.sierraclub.org/outdoors/2015/02/healing-hike-partnership

Entire Website Ⓠ

This source would entail the entire website and not just a specific page or document on the site. The reference does not have to be placed on the reference page if the full web address is included in the body of the document. The example below would appear in the text of the paper and **not** on the reference page.

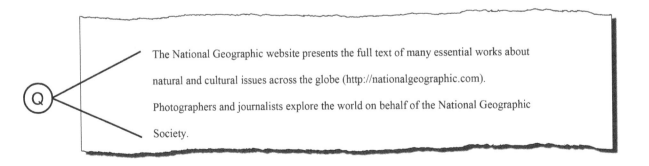

Ⓠ The National Geographic website presents the full text of many essential works about

natural and cultural issues across the globe (http://nationalgeographic.com).

Photographers and journalists explore the world on behalf of the National Geographic

Society.

Multimedia Sources (pp. 209 – 210)

For all videos, films, broadcasts, and television shows, the roles *Director, Producer, Writer, Screenwriter* should be used for the "roles" behind the author's name. If the person has more than one title (e.g., director and producer), include both in the parentheses with a backslash separating the titles (e.g., (Director/Producer)).

Videocassette/DVD/Blue-Ray Ⓡ

Producer, P. (Role), Director, D. (Role), & Writer, W. (Role) (Year). *Title* [Format]. City, State: Studio Name.

NOTE: The format should be the type of media used (e.g., DVD, Blue-Ray, or Videocassette).

Motion Picture Ⓢ

Producer, P. (Role), & Director, D. (Role). (Year). *Title* [Motion Picture]. Country: Studio.

Television Broadcast Ⓣ

Producer, P. (Role). (Year, Month Day). *Title* [Television broadcast]. City State: New Agency.

Television Show (from a Series) Ⓤ

Writer, W. (Role), & Director, D. (Role). (Year, Month Day). Episode Title [Television series episode]. In
    Producer, P. (Role), *Series title*, City, State: Studio

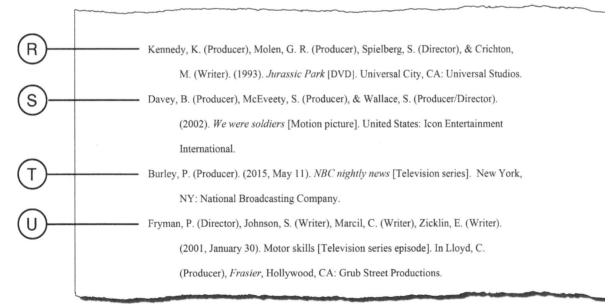

Ⓡ — Kennedy, K. (Producer), Molen, G. R. (Producer), Spielberg, S. (Director), & Crichton,
    M. (Writer). (1993). *Jurassic Park* [DVD]. Universal City, CA: Universal Studios.

Ⓢ — Davey, B. (Producer), McEveety, S. (Producer), & Wallace, S. (Producer/Director).
    (2002). *We were soldiers* [Motion picture]. United States: Icon Entertainment
    International.

Ⓣ — Burley, P. (Producer). (2015, May 11). *NBC nightly news* [Television series]. New York,
    NY: National Broadcasting Company.

Ⓤ — Fryman, P. (Director), Johnson, S. (Writer), Marcil, C. (Writer), Zicklin, E. (Writer).
    (2001, January 30). Motor skills [Television series episode]. In Lloyd, C.
    (Producer), *Frasier*, Hollywood, CA: Grub Street Productions.

Audio Recording Ⓥ

Speaker, S. (Speaker). (Year). *Title: Subtitle*. [Format]. City, State: Distributor.

NOTE: The format should be the type of media used (e.g., Cassette Recording, MP3 File, Vinyl Record, Compact Disc – can also use CD).

Music Recording Ⓦ

Songwriter, S. (Year). Song Title. On *Album Title* [Format]. City, State: Studio.

NOTE: The format should be the type of media used (e.g., Cassette Recording, MP3, Compact Disc).

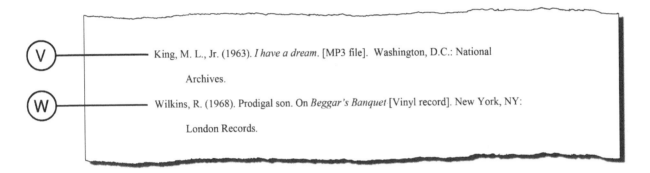

Ⓥ — King, M. L., Jr. (1963). *I have a dream*. [MP3 file]. Washington, D.C.: National Archives.

Ⓦ — Wilkins, R. (1968). Prodigal son. On *Beggar's Banquet* [Vinyl record]. New York, NY: London Records.

Personal Communication (p. 179)

Interviews, Email, or Other Personal Communication

This reference should not be placed on the reference page. Only in-text citations are included for personal communication. In parentheses, either include the name of the person (first initial, middle initial, then last name) followed by a comma, then the words *personal communication*, and the full date of the correspondence Ⓧ or if the name is included in the sentence, then only include the words personal communication and the full date Ⓨ.

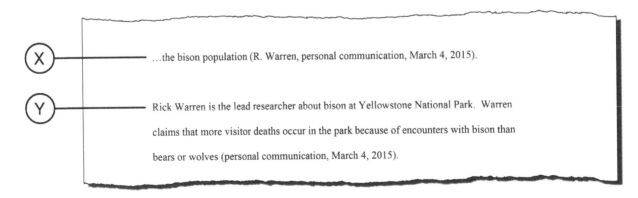

Ⓧ — …the bison population (R. Warren, personal communication, March 4, 2015).

Ⓨ — Rick Warren is the lead researcher about bison at Yellowstone National Park. Warren claims that more visitor deaths occur in the park because of encounters with bison than bears or wolves (personal communication, March 4, 2015).

Table of Contents

Since most scholarly writing is submitted to journals, the *APA Publication Manual* does not provide information about tables of contents. Universities, instructors, and specific programs should provide details about how a table of contents should appear, if it is required for an assignment. The general guidelines for a table of contents are provided below as a basis for its appearance. If a table of contents is required for an assignment, ask your instructor for guidelines.

The running head Ⓐ and page number Ⓑ are included in the header. When a table of contents is included, all pages between the title page and the first page of the manuscript are numbered with small roman numerals (e.g., i, ii, iii, iv, v, vi, …). The title *Table of Contents* Ⓒ is centered in bold in Times New Roman font at 12-point. All entries in the Table of Contents Ⓔ are double-spaced in Times New Roman font at 12-point. There should be an entry for every heading in the paper. Each heading level is indented five spaces from the previous heading level. The reference section and appendices are considered Level I headings and appear in the table of contents. All page numbers are right justified (use full justify to align the entries on the left with the page numbers on the right) and have a series of periods between the entry and page number in order to aid in reader the table Ⓓ. (Set up the tabs on the page to include the periods between the heading and page number.) If an entry extends beyond the first line Ⓓ, indent the second line to continue the entry and then list the page number.

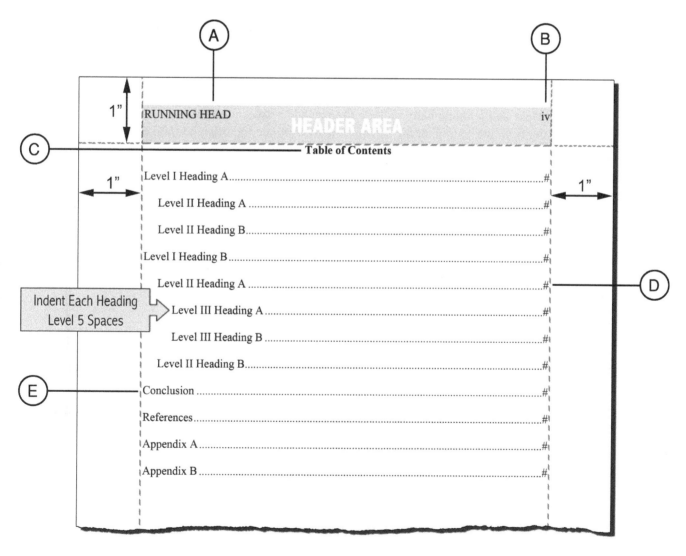

List of Tables

If a table of contents is included, then a list of tables is usually the first entry, if tables appear in your text. The list of tables also appears in journals and other academic writing, even when a table of contents is not required. The list of tables is a comprehensive list of all of the tables included in your manuscript. It appears after the table of contents (or after the title page or abstract if the table of contents is excluded) and is formatted similarly to the table of contents. All tables are listed in the order in which they appear in your manuscript. There should be an entry for every table in the paper. The title number and title that appear above the table in the text must be included in the list of tables.

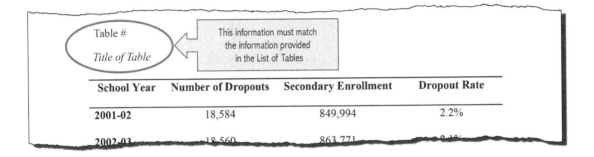

The running head Ⓐ and page number Ⓑ are included in the header. When a list of tables is included, the page number is usually listed as a lowercase Roman numeral (e.g., i, ii, iii, iv, v, vi, …). The title *List of Tables* Ⓒ is centered in bold in Times New Roman font at 12-point. All entries in the list of tables Ⓓ are double-spaced in Times New Roman font at 12-point. All page numbers are right justified and have a series of periods between the entry and page number in order to aid in reader the table Ⓓ (use tabs to align the entries on the left with the page numbers on the right and automatically include the periods between the title and page number). If a table title extends beyond the first line Ⓓ, indent the second line to continue the title and then list the page number.

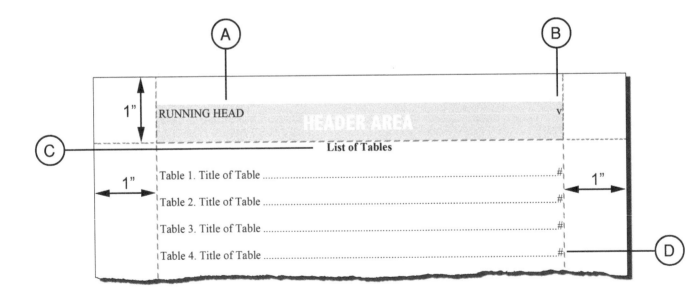

List of Figures

If a table of contents is included, then a list of figures is usually the second entry, if figures appear in your text. The list of figures also appears in journals and other academic writing, even when a table of contents is not required. The list of figures is a comprehensive list of all of the figures included in your manuscript. It appears after the list of tables and is formatted similarly to the table of contents and table of figures. All figures are listed in the order in which they appear in your manuscript. The running head Ⓐ and page number Ⓑ are included in the header. When a list of tables is included, the page number is usually listed as a lowercase Roman numeral (e.g., i, ii, iii, iv, v, vi, …). The title *List of Tables* Ⓒ is centered in bold in Times New Roman font at 12-point. All entries in the list of tables Ⓔ are double-spaced in Times New Roman font at 12-point. If a figure title extends beyond the first line Ⓓ, indent the second line to continue the title and then list the page number. There should be an entry for every figure in the paper. The figure number and title that appears below the table in the text must be included in the list of tables in the same order as they appear in the manuscript.

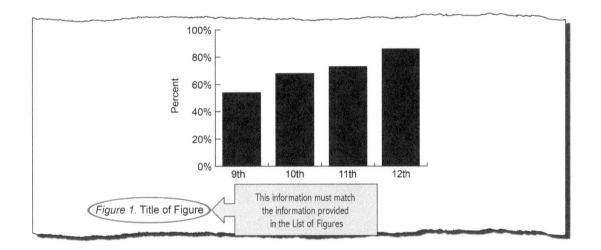

Figure 1. Title of Figure

This information must match the information provided in the List of Figures

All page numbers are right justified (use full justify to align the entries on the left with the page numbers on the right) and have a series of periods between the entry and page number in order to aid in reader the table Ⓓ.

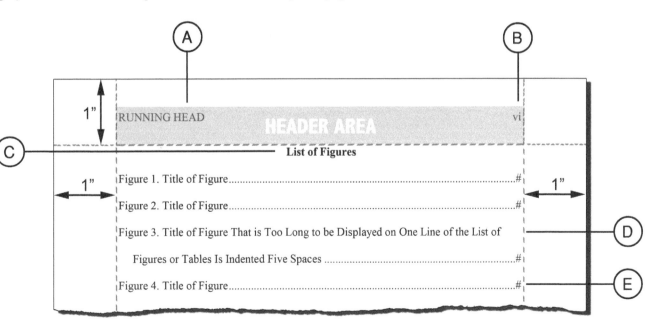

Appendices

(p. 39) Information that you need to include with your manuscript, but not within the text of the manuscript can be placed in the appendices. This information ⓔ can include raw data, surveys, instruments, calculations, consent forms, related correspondence, and any other information pertinent to the paper. If tables or text are included in the appendices, they should follow all text conventions (e.g., font, text size, spacing). Each item should have its own appendix or be grouped with similar items. For example, you may have the following appendices in a paper:

- Appendix A: Letters of Consent
- Appendix B: Permission to Conduct the Study
- Appendix C: Institutional Review Board (IRB) Approval
- Appendix D: Raw Data

If only have one appendix is added, it should be titled *Appendix*. If two or more appendices are added, they should be titled *Appendix A*, *Appendix B*, and continue on as needed ⓒ. The appendices must be referenced in the manuscript and should be included in the same order as they are referenced in the paper. The title is centered at the top of the page in bold, Times New Roman at 12-point. After skipping a line, include a title ⓓ that describes what is in the appendix. The title should be centered and in Times New Roman at 12-point. The page should have the same running header as the manuscript ⓐ and a page number ⓑ. Appendices are located behind all other components of the paper, including the reference list.

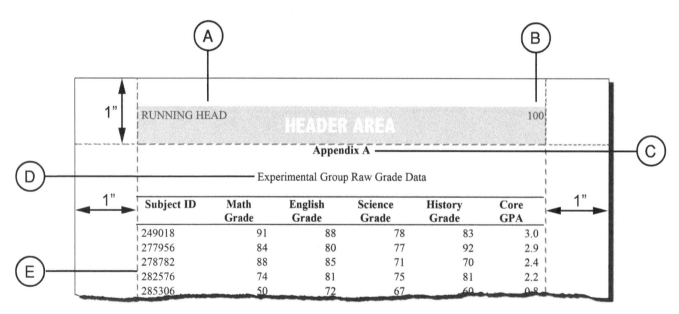

Assembling a Paper

The figure below shows the progression of the pages in a typical paper. Check to ensure that this format meets the requirements set forth by your school. If your assignment does not require one or more of the components shown, simply skip that component and continue with the remaining items. For example, a short paper may only consist of the title page, body of the paper, and references. Create or download a template to ensure that your paper is formatted and assembled correctly. A template will allow you to save time each time you write a paper.

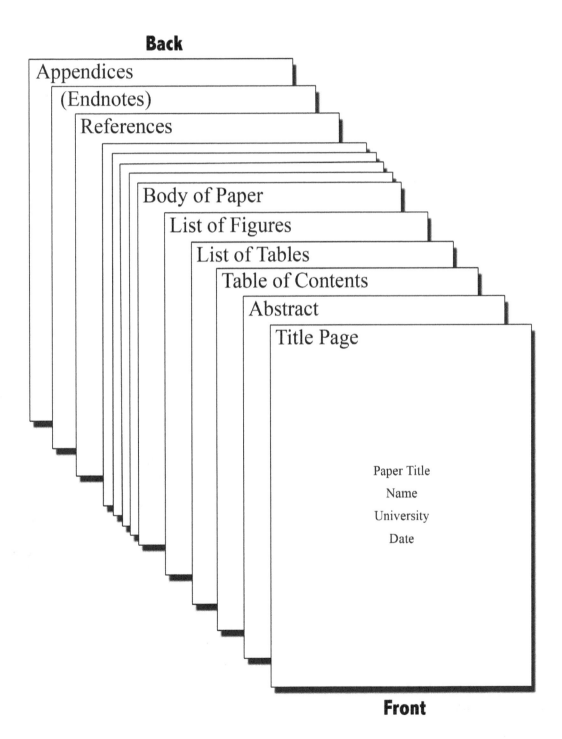

Avoiding Plagiarism

One of the most important, and often most difficult, aspects of learning is avoiding plagiarism. Plagiarism is a growing epidemic in the educational community, and schools and universities take extensive measures to detect and address plagiarism regardless if the infraction was malicious or unintended. The best defense against plagiarism is understanding the basic rules of academic writing. These basic rules are outlined below.

The information and ideas of others that is presented in your work must be properly cited and referenced. Any ideas, conclusions, theories, methods, or processes that others have created or referenced must be documented as their work and not yours. Options for sharing other people's research and writing include:

- Paraphrase, or rewrite, another author's phrases in your own words. This should be done whenever possible (see page 12).
- If you use another author's specific phrases, you must place those words in quotation marks or a block quote (see page 9).
- If you include general information that is considered to be common knowledge, you do not have to cite the source. This information could include dates of historical events, birth and death dates of well known figures (e.g., politicians, researchers, athletes, etc...). If you directly quote this information from another source (e.g., use their words to introduce common knowledge information) you must consider this to be a referenced source.
- Field-specific common knowledge can also be included without citations as long as the information is not from other author's materials.

In any of the above cases, if you are not sure if the information is common knowledge, cite and reference the source to ensure that others' are properly credited. In a paper you must cite any idea that is not yours:

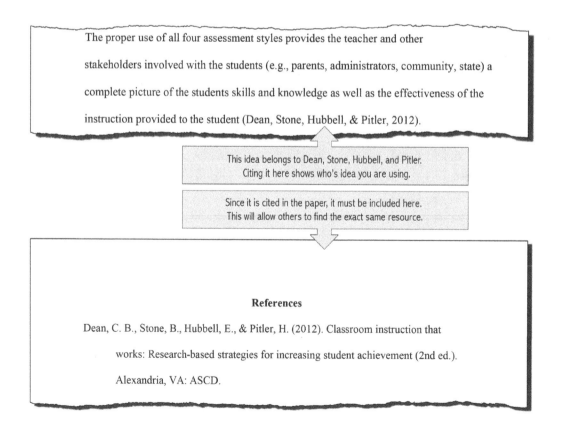

The proper use of all four assessment styles provides the teacher and other stakeholders involved with the students (e.g., parents, administrators, community, state) a complete picture of the students skills and knowledge as well as the effectiveness of the instruction provided to the student (Dean, Stone, Hubbell, & Pitler, 2012).

This idea belongs to Dean, Stone, Hubbell, and Pitler. Citing it here shows who's idea you are using.

Since it is cited in the paper, it must be included here. This will allow others to find the exact same resource.

References

Dean, C. B., Stone, B., Hubbell, E., & Pitler, H. (2012). Classroom instruction that works: Research-based strategies for increasing student achievement (2nd ed.). Alexandria, VA: ASCD.